Joy! Joy! Joy!
The Anthem for Black Boys

By Nzinga-Christina Reid, LMSW
Illustrated by Howard Barry

Dedicated to
Lutalo Isaac Reid
My Joy

BLACK BOY JOY

I've got Joy
on the inside of me

I look in the mirror
and Like what I see.

From my kinky hair
to my nose, lips, and eyes

I am a King
though I'm small in size.

Joy, Joy, Joy
All over me!

This Black boy's Joy means, I Love Me

I'll change the world with my own two hands

It's not too hard
I know
I Can!

I am so smart and Capable too

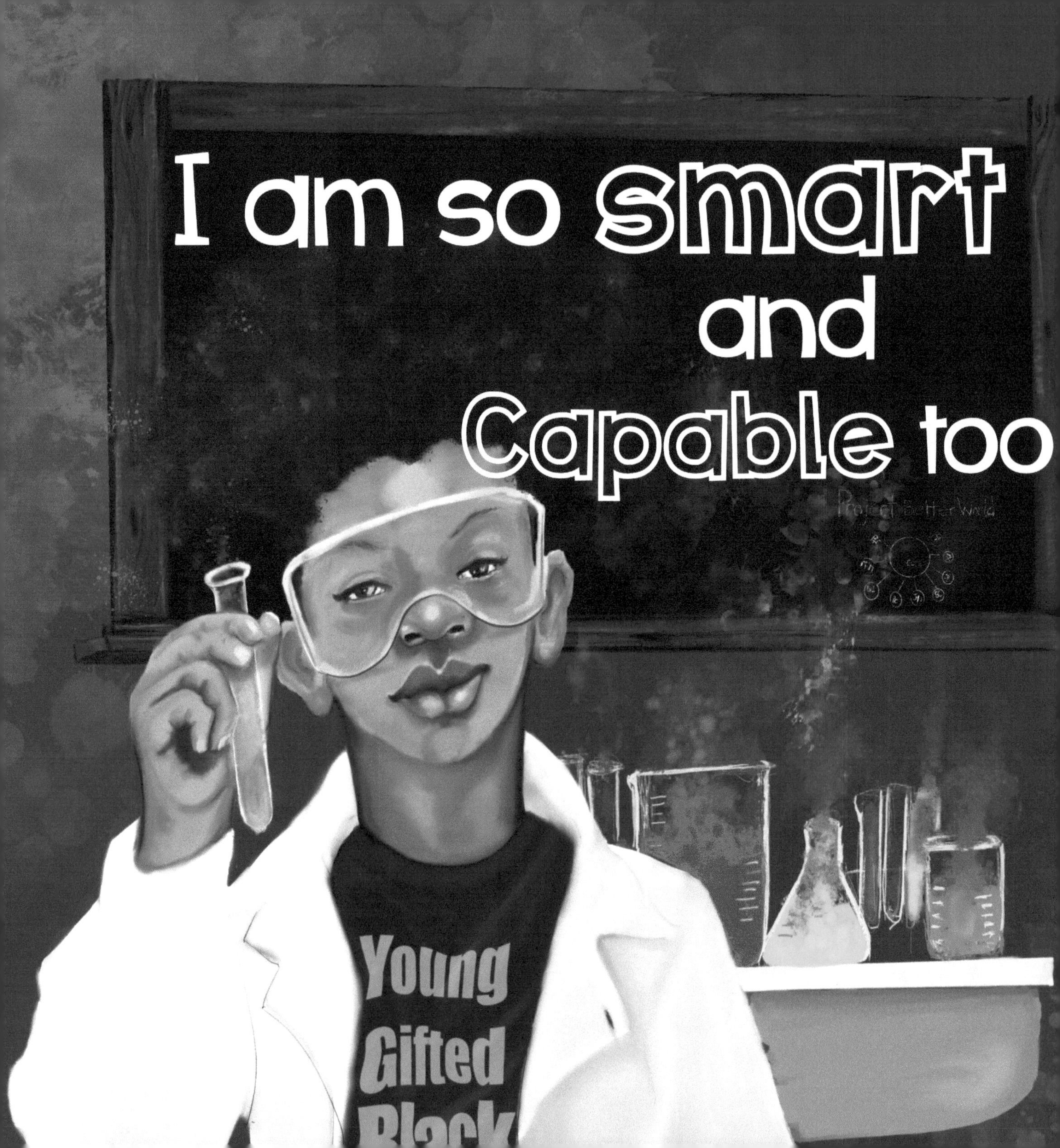

Just Unstoppable in all that I do!

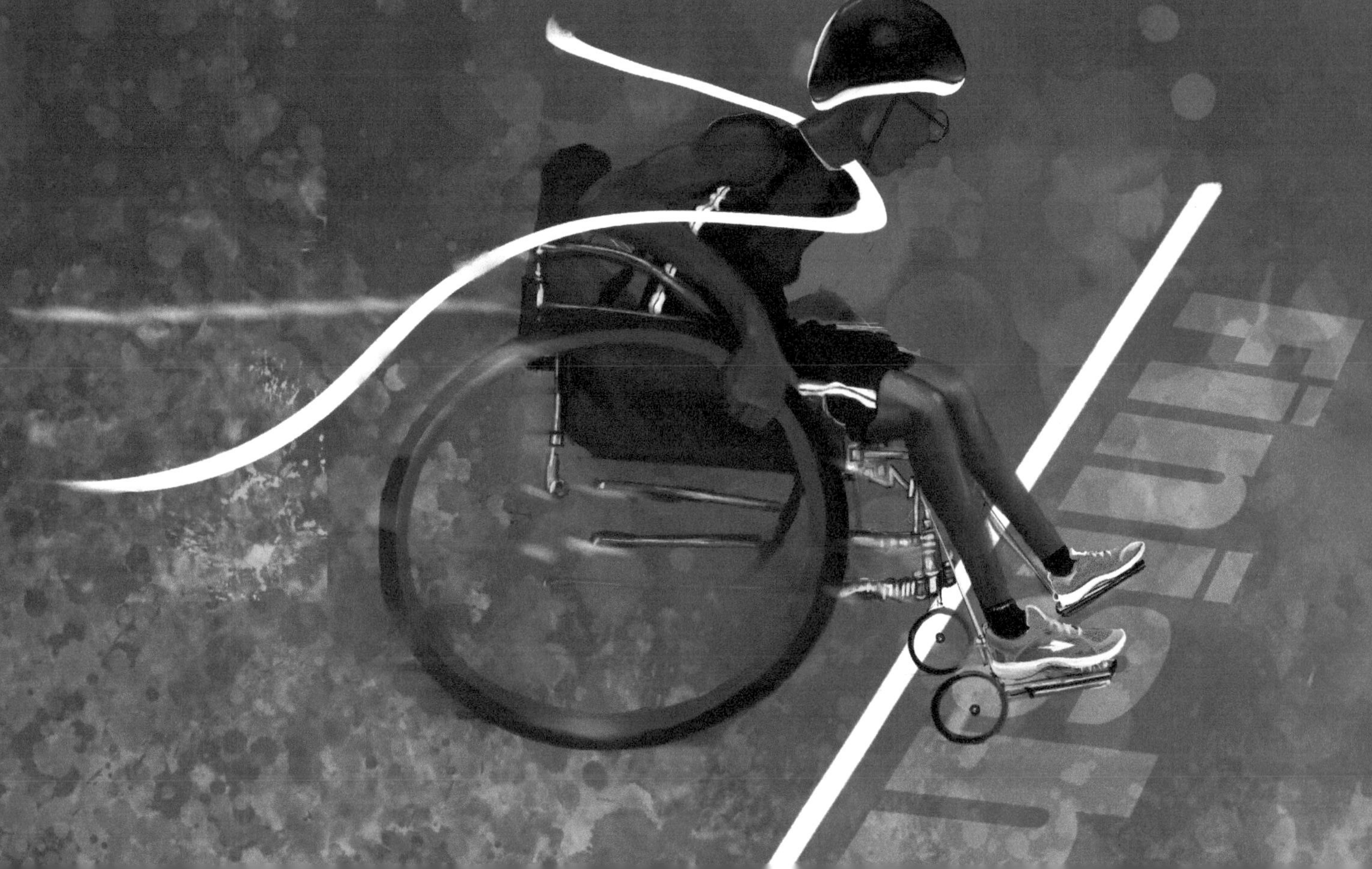

I'll do my part to protect my brothers

Let's not forget the Sisters, too

My ♥ Sisters

I'll show them Love for all they do.

Joy, Joy, Joy
All over me

This Black boy's Joy means Unity

I may fall down when times get tough

But I am strong
I'll get back
Up!

You can't stop me so don't you try.

I am
Powerful
in all that
I do

I'll speak my **Goals** and **watch** them come **true.**

And when
in doubt
or even
Afraid

I'll think of
this Anthem
and here's what
I'll say

Joy, Joy Joy
All over
Me

This Black boy's Joy
means I Love me

This Black boy's Joy
the World will see

This Black boy's Joy
means I am

Free

CPSIA information can be obtained
at www.ICGtesting.com
Printed in the USA
BVHW021914171021
619163BV00011B/48